ALSO BY RICHARD A. POSNER

Not a Suicide Pact

Uncertain Shield

Preventing Surprise Attacks

Catastrophe

Law, Pragmatism, and Democracy

Economic Analysis of Law

Frontiers of Legal Theory

Antitrust Law

The Problematics of Moral and Legal Theory

An Affair of State

Overcoming Law

Sex and Reason

The Problems of Jurisprudence

The Economics of Justice

The Little Book of Plagiarism

The Little Book of Plagiarism

Richard A. Posner

Pantheon Books, New York

All rights reserved. Published in the United States by Pantheon
Books, a division of Random House, Inc., New York, and in
Canada by Random House of Canada Limited, Toronto.

Pantheon Books and colophon are registered trademarks of
Random House, Inc.

Library of Congress Cataloging-in-Publication Data
Posner, Richard A.
The little book of plagiarism / Richard A. Posner.
p.   cm.
Includes bibliographical references.
ISBN: 978-0-375-42475-5
1. Plagiarism.   I. Title.
K1485.P67 2007
346.04'82—dc22   2006024449

www.pantheonbooks.com

Printed in the United States of America

First Edition

2 4 6 8 9 7 5 3

For Charlene

Pereant qui ante nos nostra dixerent.

Perish those who said our good things
before we did.

—Donatus

The Little Book
of Plagiarism

I

AT AGE SEVENTEEN, Kaavya Viswanathan signed a two-book contract with Little, Brown. The publisher agreed to give her an advance of $500,000 against royalties, and she sold movie rights to the books to Dreamworks for an undisclosed sum. By the time the first book, *How Opal Mehta Got Kissed, Got Wild, and Got a Life,* was published in April 2006, she was nineteen and a sophomore at Harvard. Within weeks the *Harvard Crimson* discovered and the mainstream media proclaimed far and wide that her book reproduced almost verbatim many passages from similar "chick-lit" novels by an established author, Megan McCafferty. A company engaged in the heretofore obscure trade of "book packaging" had helped Viswanathan to "conceptualize and plot" her book, but there is no indication that the company shares responsibility for her plagiarisms.

The *Crimson* listed thirteen plagiarized passages, such as the following. Viswanathan:

Priscilla was my age and lived two blocks away. For the first fifteen years of my life, those were the only qualifications I needed in a best friend. We had first bonded over our mutual fascination with the abacus in a playgroup for gifted kids. But that was before freshman year, when Priscilla's glasses came off, and the first in a long string of boyfriends got on.

McCafferty:

Bridget is my age and lives across the street. For the first twelve years of my life, these qualifications were all I needed in a best friend. But that was before Bridget's braces came off and her boyfriend Burke got on, before Hope and I met in our seventh-grade honors classes.

Viswanathan at first denied everything, then claimed that the copying was "unconscious"—that she had "internalized" McCafferty's novels (which she admitted having read). She had a photographic memory, she said, though not for the copying itself. At first, Little, Brown said it would republish the book without the offending passages. But after Viswanathan was discovered to have copied material for her novel from other authors besides McCafferty, including Salman Rushdie, the publisher recalled the book and canceled its contract with her.

What was Viswanathan thinking when she plagiarized? The Associated Press has revealed that she had been "featured in a 2004 *Chronicle of Higher Education* article detailing how even successful students are 'schmoozing' with [college] admissions officials to make themselves more memorable. Viswanathan was described as having visited nine exclusive colleges, following up with phone calls and monthly e-mails to admissions officers to underscore her interest. 'I think a lot of applying to college is about strategy,' Viswanathan told the magazine. 'When they read my application, maybe they'll remember me.' " Apparently Harvard did. Strategy made her, and in the end strategy undid her.

Here is a kindlier explanation. In an age of specialization (perhaps in any age, as Harold Bloom argued in *The Anxiety of Influence*), a creative person is apt to have a feeling of belatedness—a feeling that though just as creative as his predecessors he has appeared on the scene too late; the ship has sailed; the niche he might have filled has been filled already. Oh, the unfairness, Viswanathan might have thought, of McCafferty's having picked the low-hanging "chick-lit" fruit rather than leaving some of it for her.

Newspaper readers might think plagiarism a Harvard specialty. Doris Kearns Goodwin, who had taught part-time at Harvard for a decade and was a member of the university's Board of Overseers, and three Harvard law professors—Laurence Tribe, Charles Ogletree, and Alan Dershowitz—had recently been accused, along with sophomore Viswanathan. Goodwin, as we'll see, made an incomplete and misleading confession—and was quickly rehabilitated (though plagiarists, I shall argue, are never *completely* rehabilitated). Tribe confessed and received a mild reprimand from his dean. In Ogletree's case the plagiarism was by a research assistant. His appears to have been a "managed book," in which the (nominal) author is mainly the editor of others' prose. Ogletree received undisclosed discipline, but was not fired. Dershowitz, a prominent Zionist, was accused by anti-Zionists of citing primary sources without acknowledging that he had found the references to them in secondary sources that he did not cite. He denied the accusation, and that was the end of the matter.

One doubts that plagiarism is actually more common at Harvard than elsewhere. It is simply more conspicuous. Scandal at the nation's most famous university gratifies the natural human delight at discovering that giants, including giant institutions, have feet of clay.

Plagiarism, as the Viswanathan affair shows,

can be a gaudy offense. It can also be a fabricated one. The suit for copyright and trademark infringement that Nancy Stouffer brought against J. K. Rowling, the author of the Harry Potter books, was so lacking in merit—the suit was found to have been based in part on forged and altered documents—that the court imposed a $50,000 penalty on Stouffer. Plagiarism has sometimes a comical air, as when the University of Oregon plagiarized the section of Stanford's teaching-assistant handbook dealing with—plagiarism. Both Jonathan Swift and Laurence Sterne denounced plagiarism in words plagiarized from earlier writers.

It is also an offense regularly committed by celebrities, though most plagiarists are obscure—in fact most are students; an estimated one-third of all high-school and college students have committed plagiarism or a closely related form of academic fraud, such as purchasing a term paper from a "paper mill." Still, a number of prominent, even illustrious, figures are confessed or proven plagiarists, including—besides Sterne, Swift, Samuel Coleridge, and countless other literary authors—Martin Luther King Jr., Senator Joseph Biden, and Vladimir Putin. Another Vladimir—Nabokov—has been accused of plagiarism, though, I shall argue, unjustly.

Plagiarism is attracting increasing attention, though whether this is because it is becoming more common, or because its boundaries are becoming vague and contested, or because it is being detected more often (digitization has made it at once easier to commit and easier to detect) are among the many questions about it that call for investigation. What makes plagiarism a fascinating subject and the occasion for this book is the ambiguity of the concept, its complex relations to other disapproved practices of copying, including copyright infringement, the variety of its applications, its historical and cultural relativity, its contested normative significance, the mysterious motives and curious excuses of its practitioners, the means of detection, and the forms of punishment and absolution. I shall analyze these issues from a perspective shaped by my long-standing interest, both as a judge and as an academic, in the law and economics of intellectual property.

I I

To GET STARTED, we need a definition. But "plagiarism" turns out to be difficult to define. A typical dictionary definition is "literary theft." The definition is incomplete because there can be plagiarism of music, pictures, or ideas, as well as of verbal matter, though most of the time I'll assume that the plagiarist is a writer. The definition is also inaccurate; we'll see that there can be plagiarism without theft. And it is imprecise, because it is unclear what should count as "theft" when one is not taking anything away from someone but simply making a copy. When you "steal" a passage from a book, the author and his readers still have the book, unlike when you steal his car. The use of words such as *theft* and *piracy* to describe unauthorized copying is misleading. But "borrowing," the term preferred by apologists for plagiarism (and there are such apologists), is misleading, too, since the "borrowed" matter is never returned.

Obviously, not all copying is plagiarism—not even all unlawful copying, that is, copyright infringement. There is considerable overlap between plagiarism and copyright infringement, but not all plagiarism is copyright infringement and not all copyright infringement is plagiarism.

Copyrights have limited terms; after a copyright expires, the work enters the public domain and can be copied by anyone, without legal liability. And not all expressive works are copyrighted in the first place; for example, the federal government is forbidden by statute to claim copyright in the documents it produces. Had Megan McCafferty's copyrights expired, Viswanathan would not have been guilty of infringing copyright—but she would still have been a plagiarist because she concealed the copying.

Copyright law does not forbid the copying of ideas (broadly defined to include many features of an expressive work besides its precise words or other expressive details, such as genre, basic narrative structure, and theme or message), or of facts. Only the *form* in which the ideas or the facts are expressed is protected. So Dan Brown, the author of *The Da Vinci Code,* who was sued for copyright infringement by the authors of an earlier book on the grounds that he'd stolen their idea of Jesus Christ having married Mary Magdalene and fathered children by her, won the suit.

The line between idea and expression is often indistinct, however. How loose must a paraphrase be to escape infringing? (That is also an issue with plagiarism.) Copying a generic plot or a stock character from a novelist, or historical facts from a historian, is not copyright infringement. But copying details of plot, as Brown arguably did, and of character could well be. If, however, the plot clearly is generic, the character clearly a stock character, the historical facts already known, the arrangement of the work familiar or inevitable (for example, a historical account arranged chronologically), and any scientific or other abstract ideas already familiar to the intended readership, there is no copyright infringement.

There is also no infringement if a coauthor licenses the reproduction of the copyrighted work without consulting the other author(s) of it, though he will have to split the license fee with them. And subject to the same duty to share the profits, he can use the coauthored work in his own future writings without his coauthors' permission. Yet there would be plagiarism if the coauthored material that was copied into a new work without acknowledgment had actually been written by one of the other authors.

There can likewise be plagiarism when non-copyrightable features of a work (whether or not the work is copyrighted) are copied without acknowledgment, so that readers of the new work are invited to think that those features are the invention or discovery of the plagiarist. This kind of plagiarism can take quite subtle forms.

For example, a historian might cite a primary source that he had not found or read himself but rather had lifted from a citation in a secondary source that he does not mention, thus appropriating the discovery made by the author of the secondary work. This is the form of plagiarism of which Professor Dershowitz was accused. It is a common practice (as well as an old one— Ben Jonson was accused of it), especially in law review articles, because law professors are mad for citing and, as we'll see, originality is not highly prized in law. It is a common practice because its consequences are too trivial to arouse much ire (Dershowitz's accusers had ulterior motives) and because, unless the primary source is exceedingly obscure or downright inaccessible or the secondary source contains an error in citing the primary source that is carried over into the accused plagiarist's citation, it is almost impossible to detect. But is it really plagiarism, or an example of the fuzziness of the concept? For it's not so much a matter of copying as of falsely implying that one did the drudge work (sometimes more than drudge work) of digging up the primary sources.

Some commentators on the Viswanathan affair have pointed out that copyright law allows some unauthorized word-for-word copying of copyrighted works under the rubric of "fair use," and they infer from this that some plagiarism, maybe even hers, might not be copyright infringement. The fair-use doctrine permits quotation of brief passages from a copyrighted work without the copyright holder's permission. The reason is that such limited copying does the author no harm except to deprive him of the trivial fee that he might extract from the copier were there no right of fair use—a fee that would probably be smaller than the costs in time and postage (or equivalent) of negotiating for the right.

But the fair user is assumed to use quotation marks and credit the source; he is not a plagiarist. I thus disagree that there can be "fair use" when the copier is passing off the copied passage as his own. The fair-use right is an exception to copyright, which normally prohibits the unauthorized publication of copyrighted work, and why should the exception shelter plagiarists? The plagiarist does not play fair. Were there such an exception, one could write a book consisting entirely of unacknowledged passages from other writers, provided one took only a small amount from each work; in fact it would be a case of both plagiarism and copyright infringement.

The law does not excuse copyright infringement, no matter how fulsome the infringer's acknowledgment of his copying; but the acknowledgment will exonerate him of any charge of plagiarism. Or at least should—because judges will sometimes call copyright infringers "plagiarists" though there is no concealment. This loose usage erases what is distinctive about plagiarism, though it illustrates how the rise of copyright has made copying a suspicious activity.

Concealment is at the heart of plagiarism. But it must be carefully defined. It is not a mere failure to acknowledge copying. Often copying is not acknowledged because it is known to the intended readership. A parody may quote extensively from the work parodied, and always it will copy distinctive features of style and theme, yet often without mentioning the parodied work. But the parodist will plant clues so numerous and unmistakable that the reader will recognize the copying, for otherwise the parody will not be recognized as a parody and the parodist's intentions will be thwarted. And often works that are not parodies nevertheless will allude to an earlier work, the allusion taking the form of a verbatim quotation from the work without quotation marks. Allusion is not plagiarism, because the reader is expected to recognize the allusion.

Sometimes there is no acknowledgment, tacit or express, of the original author but readers are indifferent; they may be deceived, but the deception has no consequences. Textbooks are an obvious example. They do not cite the sources of most of the ideas expounded in them because there is no pretense of originality—rather the contrary: the most reliable textbook is one that confines itself to ideas already well accepted by the experts in the field. And since students have little or no interest in the origins of the ideas they are studying, source references would merely clutter the exposition. Moreover, the originators of the ideas expounded in a textbook seek recognition not from students but from their peers. Einstein would not have been upset to learn that some high-school physics students thought the author of their textbook had discovered the theory of relativity. Textbook authors are guilty of plagiarism not when they copy ideas without acknowledgment, but only when they copy verbal passages without acknowledgment.

A judgment of plagiarism requires that the copying, besides being deceitful in the sense of misleading the intended readers, induce *reliance* by them. By this I mean that the reader does something because he thinks the plagiarizing work original that he would not have done had he known the truth. (Lawyers call this "detrimental" reliance, that is, relying to your detriment on a falsehood.) He buys a book that he wouldn't have bought had he known it contained large swatches of another writer's book; he would have bought that other writer's book instead. Or if he's a teacher he gives a bad student a good grade, to the prejudice of other students in the class (if the students are graded on a curve), thinking the student's paper original.

The reader has to *care* about being deceived about authorial identity in order for the deceit to cross the line to fraud and thus constitute plagiarism. More precisely, he has to care enough that had he known he would have acted differently. There are innumerable intellectual deceits that do little or no harm because they engender little or no reliance. They arouse not even tepid moral indignation, and so they escape the plagiarism label. Most nonlawyers probably think judges write their own opinions. Only a small minority of us do nowadays; the others edit their law clerks' opinion drafts to a greater or lesser extent—

sometimes so extensively that the judge deserves to be considered a coauthor or even the principal coauthor of the opinion, though not the sole author. Judges or their clerks sometimes insert into their opinions, without attribution, verbatim passages from lawyers' briefs; and many orders, findings of fact, and other documents signed by judges are actually prepared entirely by the parties' lawyers, again without attribution. Yet judges sign their opinions and orders as if they were the sole authors, and they refer to one another's opinions as if written by the judge named as the author. Judges would like people to believe they write their own opinions—which is the element of deceit, for judicial acknowledgment of ghost authorship by law clerks is vanishingly rare.

Nevertheless the publishing of a law clerk's draft under the judge's name is not plagiarism. Very few people who think judges write their own opinions would change their behavior (avoid litigation, oppose a judicial nominee, vote against a judge's retention, and so forth) if they learned the truth. And the principal readers of judicial opinions are not an ignorant laity, but legal professionals who know that most judicial opinions are largely written by law clerks. Since judges are not permitted to copyright their opinions and so obtain no royalties from them, the financial motive so perspicuous in Viswanathan's case is absent.

Then too, little value is ascribed to judicial originality—sometimes it is actually disapproved, on the grounds that it tends to destabilize law. Judges do not brag about the number of cases they have overruled, the doctrines they have slain, the doctrines they have created. They would rather be regarded as sound than as original, as appliers of law rather than inventors of it. Judges find it politic to pretend that they are the slaves of the law, never its masters and the competitors of legislators.

Law professors, too, are less than scrupulous about acknowledging the provenance of their ideas, because originality is not much prized by law professors either, though this is changing, as disparagement of intellectual adventurousness on the part of judges is not. It is changing because law professors increasingly identify with other academics, who prize originality, rather than with judges and lawyers. The transition is incomplete; many law professors continue, particularly in the legal treatises and textbooks they write, to publish without acknowledgment material drafted by their student research assistants. But the analogy between those professors and judges who publish law clerks' opinions under their own name is imperfect. Law clerks are hired on the clear understanding that they are writing for and in the name of their judge. This tends not to be the explicit understanding in the case of student research assistants. The research they do clearly belongs to the professor, but not their words.

I had thought the practice of textbook writers of incorporating without acknowledgment passages written by others a specialty of law professors until I read a recent article in the *New York Times* by Diana Schemo, which quotes a historian as saying that elementary and high school textbooks "were usually corporate-driven collaborative efforts, in which the publisher had extensive rights to hire additional writers, researchers and editors and to make major revisions without the authors' final approval." Many textbooks appear under the names of long-dead authors whose contributions to the work have been diluted to the vanishing point by an army of unnamed freelancers, in-house writers, and editors. Some textbooks are entirely ghostwritten, the nominal author being regarded as strictly a marketing tool.

The situation regarding books nominally authored by politicians and celebrities but actually ghostwritten more resembles that of judicial opinions than that of textbooks. (Celebrity blogs are the latest example of ghosted celebrity writing.) There are no victims. The ghostwriter is compensated, and since there is no expectation of originality the public is not fooled. But the increasingly common practice of identifying the ghostwriter in the book may create the impression of celebrity authorship when no ghostwriter is mentioned, as in the case of Hillary Clinton's book *It Takes a Village,* where the contract with the ghostwriter forbade disclosure of her role. Yet one cannot imagine the public caring.

In both cases, moreover, that of the judge and that of the politician or celebrity, there is a defensible rationalization for any deceit involved in their use of ghostwriters. It is that in the case of a public figure what is important is not authorship but commitment. (This is another way of saying that the public is not really fooled.) The judge by signing "his" opinions and the politician by being identified as the author of "his" book—even the movie star whose celebrity persuades the credulous that he might have something worthwhile to say about public issues—are affirming their commitment to the contents of the work. (Not so the posthumous textbook author.) Their assertion of authorship is the equivalent of a celebrity endorsement of a product. Similarly, the solicitor general of the United States signs the briefs that the federal government submits to the Supreme Court, though he does not write them. But he is not claiming authorship; he is merely making clear that he approves the brief. In the rare case in which he does not sign it, he creates a powerful signal of internal dissension regarding the government's legal position.

Rembrandt may have been doing something similar when he signed his name to paintings done entirely by his assistants: certifying them as Rembrandt-quality paintings. Rembrandt's corpus of work, like Coleridge's, has been shrinking as more and more of the paintings he signed are discovered to have been painted by other artists. But it would be odd to call Rembrandt a "plagiarist," as he was a better artist than the painters whose work he signed. What he did was fraud by modern standards because it enhanced value by means of a false pretense. But we think of plagiarism as an offense designed to make the plagiarist look better than he is, and Rembrandt was making the "plagiarized" works seem, or at least be thought (for many of the faux Rembrandts are excellent paintings even though their value nosedives when they are discovered not to be genuine Rembrandts), better than *they* were. That is like affixing a prestigious trademark to an inferior version of the trademarked product—the commonest form of trademark infringement.

Another curious example of authorship is that of the laboratory head who is listed as a coauthor of all the scholarly papers written by his staff. As Richard Lewontin, a distinguished scientist, disapprovingly explains, "Regardless of the actual involvement of the laboratory director in the intellectual and physical work of a research project, he or she has unchallenged intellectual-property rights in the project, much as a lord had unchallenged property rights in the product of serfs or peasants occupying dependent lands." It is the modern equivalent of Rubens's workshop (see Part VI).

For "authored" in the cases I have been dis-

cussing we perhaps should substitute "authorized," as in the King James Version of the Bible,
which members of the Church of England call
"The Authorized Version." James I did not write
the King James Version. Or, rather than saying
that the solicitor general is not claiming authorship when he signs the government's brief, we
might say with Michel Foucault and Roland
Barthes that "writer" and "author" are not syn-
onyms, that you can be the author of a work
though you were not the writer. Moses did not
write the five books of Moses (one of which
describes his death and burial), King David did
not write the psalms, and Saint Matthew did not
write the Gospel According to Matthew. In
ancient times it was a common convention to
assign authorship not to the actual writer of a
work but to someone whose identification with it
would lend it authority. This is again celebrity
endorsement. Of course it doesn't (or at least it
shouldn't) work when, as was probably the case
with Moses (himself possibly a fictitious rather

than real person), King David, and Saint Matthew, the celebrity is unacquainted with the work. It shouldn't work for General Omar Bradley's autobiography, almost all of which was ghostwritten after his death. In all these cases, many readers are unaware of the embarrassing fact that the nominal author had nothing (or virtually nothing, in Bradley's case) to do with the work.

Recall "book packaging," peripherally involved in the Viswanathan scandal? As explained by Jenna Glatzer,

> Nancy Drew, Sweet Valley High, Goosebumps, and many of the Complete Idiot's Guide and For Dummies series are packaged. . . . Edward Stratemeyer may have been the father of this sector of the industry. He formed a company, Stratemeyer Syndicates, to create books from his ideas. These became classic series, including The Bobbsey Twins, The Hardy Boys, and Nancy Drew. Stratemeyer hired ghostwriters to

work from his outlines, paying them a flat fee and publishing them under several pseudonyms. He also established a policy that is still used by some packagers today: authors were not allowed to talk about the books they'd written. Stratemeyer wanted to keep up the illusion that each book in a series was written by a single author, so he didn't give byline credit to the ghostwriters. Speaking about their work would have been akin to telling a child there's no Santa Claus; it would ruin the fantasy he created.

Despite the last sentence, there is no significant deception in "book packaging" as long as the packager assures reasonable uniformity among the books in each series so that the reader of the first book does not feel a jarring discontinuity when he picks up the second and subsequent volumes in the series. The pretense of a single author operates like a trademark, which often functions as a warrant of uniform quality rather than an identifier of a unique source. Coca-Cola is produced in many different bottling plants, but the trademark warrants that the product is nevertheless uniform.

Reliance and hence fraud and hence plagiarism are matters of expectation. In European countries it remains common and unexceptionable for professors to publish under their own name books and articles written by their assistants, and since that is well known in academic circles there is no fraud. It is not the practice in the United States, however, so that when Julius Kirshner, a historian at the University of Chicago, was discovered to have published under his own name a book review written by a graduate student, Kirshner was censured for plagiarism. The censure took the curious form of barring him from teaching graduate students for five years. (Undergraduates were indignant!) The *Chicago Tribune* reported Kirshner as responding oddly to his punishment by saying "I feel exonerated. There was no finding of academic fraud. I'm still teaching here."

We should try to be precise about the harm

caused by Kirshner's appropriation of his student's work. The most direct harm was to the student, presumably an aspiring academic who would have derived a career benefit had his authorship been acknowledged—which may be why he turned Kirshner in. Of course, it is possible that no journal would have published a review written by a student, but this problem could have been overcome by Kirshner's listing the student as coauthor. Readers may have been harmed by according an authority to the review that they would not have done had they known a student had written the entire review; this harm would not have been eliminated by a false attribution of coauthorship to Kirshner.

Kirshner's academic competitors may have been harmed, though surely trivially, if his plagiarism enabled him to publish more than they. In other cases, however, competitive harm is a significant consequence of plagiarism. The plagiarist by plagiarizing improves his work relative to that of his competitors and so increases his sales and his fame relative to theirs.

Solid rumor has it that the sort of thing that Kirshner did is not uncommon in academic law or limited to the writers of legal treatises. This would be consistent with the low regard in which the legal profession holds originality.

The discussion to this point enables us to define plagiarism tentatively as "fraudulent copying," which clearly distinguishes it from copyright infringement. But even this definition may not be quite right, because it is unclear that consensual copying, though it can be a fraud, should be classified as plagiarism. A student who buys his term paper from a paper mill commits an academic fraud, and if he bought the paper from an online service, which is the norm nowadays, he "copied" the paper in a literal sense. But the copying is not any sort of wrong to the author of the paper, and so "plagiarism" doesn't seem quite right. It might be better to confine the word to "nonconsensual fraudulent copying," while emphasizing that "plagiarism" does not exhaust intellectual fraud.

Fraud is a tort—a civil wrong for which damages or other legal relief can be obtained in a lawsuit—and often a crime. Plagiarism as such is neither, but the qualification in "as such" is important. Though there is no legal wrong named "plagiarism," plagiarism can become the basis of a lawsuit if it infringes copyright or breaks the contract between author and publisher. Their contract will invariably require the author to warrant the originality of the work— Little, Brown treated Viswanathan's plagiarism as a breach and canceled its contract with her in response. Other common sanctions are expulsion or other formal discipline for plagiarism by students and faculty, sanctions that although outside the conventional legal process are based ultimately on the violation of an implied contractual duty of students and faculty to their school not to commit plagiarism. The most common sanction for plagiarism by a journalist is to fire the journalist.

Plagiarism could probably be attacked in a civil lawsuit as fraud, by analogy to the tort of false advertising, if it diverted sales from competing publishers, though I am not aware of such a suit. In addition, the European doctrine of "moral rights," now gaining a foothold in U.S. law (mainly in relation to visual art), entitles a writer or other artist to be credited for his original work, and this "attribution right," as it is called, would give him a legal claim against a plagiarist. (Clumsy paraphrasing, which defaced the original, would violate another of the "moral rights"—the artist's right to insist that the integrity of his work be respected.) Attribution is important to creators of intellectual work even when there is no direct financial benefit. Authors who grant free "Creative Commons" copyright licenses for nonprofit uses often condition the grant on the licensees' acknowledging their licensors' authorship.

By far the most common punishments for plagiarism outside the school setting have nothing to do with law. They are disgrace, humiliation, ostracism, and other shaming penalties imposed by public opinion on people who violate social norms whether or not they are also legal norms. A striking example is the collapse of Senator Joseph Biden's campaign for the Democratic nomination for president in 1988 after it was revealed that he had lifted the opening paragraph of one of his campaign speeches from a campaign speech by Neil Kinnock, the leader of the British Labour Party. The reaction to Biden's conduct may seem odd, since there is no presumption that politicians write their own speeches any more than there is a presumption that stand-up comedians write their own jokes. But although a ghostwriter is not a victim of the plagiarist (if that is what one wants to call the nominal author) but his collaborator, Kinnock was not a collaborator of Biden's; he was not complicit in the copying. Yet not being a competitor of Biden either, he was not hurt by the plagiarism—on the contrary, it was a tribute to his eloquence that an American politician should have copied him and thus a true example of the adage that imitation is the sincerest form of flattery—though for all one knows Kinnock's speech had been ghostwritten.

The reaction to Biden's plagiarism was probably as strong as it was because he had introduced the plagiarized passage by saying he'd just thought of it on the way to give the speech, and because the paragraph he copied from Kinnock's speech was autobiographical, so that he seemed to be appropriating Kinnock's life rather than just his words. Another factor was that other charges of plagiarism were quickly leveled against Biden.

Almost two decades after Biden plagiarized Kinnock, the incident has been largely forgotten—yet the fact that Biden is a plagiarist has not been. The stigma of plagiarism seems never to fade completely, not because it is an especially heinous offense but because it is embarrassingly second rate; its practitioners are pathetic, almost ridiculous.

Speaking of plagiarism by politicians, Putin's plagiarism, unlike Biden's, was of the garden-variety sort. Like Martin Luther King Jr., Putin incorporated plagiarized material in an academic dissertation.

Should plagiarism be a crime or a tort? It should not be. The harms it causes are too slight to warrant cranking up the costly and clumsy machinery of the criminal law. And plagiarists rarely have sufficient assets to make suing them worthwhile, even if such harm as plagiarism does in a particular case could be monetized, which usually it could not be. Plagiarism is thus the kind of wrongdoing best left to informal, private sanctions. Despite these sanctions, there is a good deal of plagiarism, so they must be less than totally effective. But the same is true of formal legal sanctions; murder is heavily punished, but there are plenty of murders. And except in the student case, plagiarism can hardly be thought a social problem grave enough to warrant draconian solutions. It may even be a diminishing problem, especially in the student case. Although digitization has reduced the cost of committing plagiarism along one dimension—you don't have to go to a library and copy out passages by hand in order to plagiarize if you have a computer and access to the Web—it has increased it along another. For we shall see that the advent of powerful plagiarism-detection software is increasing the detectability, and hence the expected punishment cost, of plagiarism.

Curiously, most litigation over plagiarism is instituted by rather than against students expelled or otherwise disciplined for committing plagiarism. The ingenious legal theories spun by the student litigants run the gamut from breach of contract to denial of due process of law (if the school is a public institution). The threat of litigation makes some academic administrators gun-shy about expelling students caught plagiarizing.

III

VIEWING PLAGIARISM as a form of fraud and hence as dependent on inducing reliance by readers or other audience for the plagiarizing work can help us distinguish plagiaristic from non-plagiaristic copying. It can also help us grade the severity of the different forms of plagiarism, and thus design an appropriately graduated scale of punishments, though the amount and character of the reliance induced by the plagiarist are not the only things relevant to judging the gravity of his offense. His state of mind is also important, and likewise detectability, which turns out to be related to state of mind.

Reliance is the key to evaluating "self-plagiarism." If you assign away your copyright without reserving a right to republish the copyrighted work, you are guilty of copyright infringement even though you're just copying yourself. But are you also guilty of plagiarism? If so, the guilt is very widespread. William Landes and I, in our book *The Economic Structure of Intellectual Property Law,* give the following examples:

> Gilbert Stuart is reported to have painted some 75 substantially similar portraits of George Washington. Giorgio de Chirico made numerous copies of many of his best-known early Surrealist works. . . . Yeats and Auden revised their poems many years after original publication and published the revised versions in collections of their work. A recent review of a variorum edition of poems by Coleridge notes Coleridge's "revisionary obsession," which resulted for example in there being 18 different *published* versions of *The Ancient Mariner.*

Here is an example to test one's intuitions about self-plagiarism: Laurence Sterne, whose great novel *Tristram Shandy* copies extensively and without acknowledgment from other authors, also sent letters to his mistress that he had copied years earlier from letters he'd written to his wife. That was gross behavior, but was it plagiarism? No harm was done, and there may have been value created: Sterne may have thought that the letters to his wife contained his most heartfelt and eloquent declarations of love; that he couldn't improve on them and if nevertheless he composed new letters to his mistress they would be inferior and thus fail to convey his ardor. Of course, wife and mistress would have been furious had they found out. They would have thought Sterne lazy, exploitive, and insincere. Yet it would not have been the copying that bothered them but what the copying revealed about his character. His plagiarism could do no harm to anybody; only the discovery of it could.

Even if we set so special a case to one side, it is hard to see how copying yourself hurts anybody, except possibly yourself by undermining the market for your plagiarized works. Self-copying becomes fraudulent and therefore plagiaristic only when the author represents his latest work to be newly composed when in fact it is a copy of an earlier work of his that readers may have read. (Suppose the only change he has made is in the title—or in the author's name.) It is like a shop that deliberately bills a customer twice for the same item. Yet readers should realize that authors repeat themselves; it is only wholesale and literal repetition that should disappoint.

Here is another curious, though unproven, example to test one's intuitions about plagiarism. Margaret Truman, President Truman's daughter, is widely believed to have sold the use of her name to one or more professional mystery writers, who wrote and published mysteries "by Margaret Truman" without acknowledgment of their role. (The tennis player Martina Navratilova, the "author" of mystery novels about a female tennis player who solves crimes, has, in contrast, been open about the fact that the novels are ghostwritten.) Those were more innocent times, and I imagine that virtually all readers believed that Margaret Truman had actually written the mysteries attributed to her. Some readers would have been indignant had they learned otherwise (another case where a harm results not from the plagiarism but from its discovery). Would that have been a justified reaction? Obviously Ms. Truman was not harming the "plagiarized" authors—they consented to and were compensated for the deception. As for readers attracted to the books by the celebrity of the "author" and perhaps the oddness of presidential offspring writing mysteries (the wonder is not that it is done well, but that it is done at all, as Samuel Johnson famously said in a different context), they might have been angered had they discovered the deception. But it is hard to see how they were hurt by the deception itself. Did they forgo reading better mysteries? But they did not read the Truman books in expectation that these were superior mysteries by virtue of their authorship. Margaret Truman had no reputation as a writer except what the mysteries themselves created. No one could have thought that by virtue of being the president's daughter she must be an expert judge of mysteries, whose "endorsement" would therefore carry weight. (Though maybe they thought that as a Washington insider she would bring something special to mystery writing.)

Yet there were victims of the deception, which was therefore (if it really occurred, which, as I said, has not been proved) fraudulent. They were neither the readers nor the writers of her books. They were other mystery writers, who lost sales to readers attracted to the Truman books by the celebrity of the supposed author. The parallel is to textbooks whose named authors did not write them, and to students who copy the papers of other students with their consent. The harm in the first case is to the authors of competing textbooks, and in the second case to other students in the class. But just as in the rumored case of Margaret Truman, there is no "theft," no involuntary taking.

That is also true, by the way, of fabrication. It

involves no copying, and no one would call it plagiarism. But it is literary deceit, has consequences similar to those of plagiarism, and, particularly in journalism and science, is frequently conjoined with plagiarism—the case of Jayson Blair, the young *New York Times* reporter whose exposure as a fabricator-cum-plagiarist rocked the newspaper and caused two of its senior executives, including the executive editor, Howell Raines, to be fired. The conjunction is not surprising. A journalist who wants to spice up his articles can do so by making up colorful facts as well as by copying from an abler writer, and a scientist can try to steal a march on his competitors by plagiarizing another scientist but also by cooking the results of his own experiments.

We should now be able to see that even when plagiarism and copyright infringement overlap, they are different wrongs in the sense of injuring different interests of the victims. Copyright infringement is the invasion of a property right. It is like joyriding, that is, "renting" a car without paying any rent. It reduces the income of the owner of the copied work. Nothing like that is involved when a student plagiarizes, or when the plagiarized work is not in copyright (so that anyone is free to copy it), or when that work, whether or not it is copyrighted, does not compete with the work that plagiarizes it. But competitors *of the plagiarist* may still be harmed in the last case, as also in the student case. And notice that the *talented* writer who plagiarizes, whether he is a professional writer or a student, may make his work much better, and this will make the harm to his nonplagiarizing competitors, the other writers or students, even greater.

But couldn't the student plagiarist himself also be thought a victim? He derives no educational benefit from the assignment that he completed by copying another's work. No *educational benefit,* or at least no *direct* educational benefit. But if he gets a better grade than he would have gotten had he not plagiarized, or if he uses the time saved by plagiarizing to do more work on another assignment that interests him more, he may derive in the first case a career benefit and in the second case an actual educational benefit. If student plagiarism were irrational, there would be much less of it.

Although I have emphasized the differences between plagiarism and copyright infringement, plagiarism that also infringes copyright is more reprobated than plagiarism that does not. Plagiarism that infringes copyright adds a clear legal violation to an ethical violation and by invading a property right usually does more harm to the author of the copied work.

I V

WITH PLAGIARISM UNDERSTOOD as fraudulent
copying and fraud tied to reliance and hence to
expectations, it becomes easy to understand the
extraordinary historical and cultural variability of
the concept, and indeed its variability even within
a specific historical and cultural milieu. In modern America, as we know, publishing a judicial
opinion under the name of the judge who did
not write it is not plagiarism, but a professor's
publishing an article actually written by his student research assistant is.

The concept of plagiarism is often thought to
be modern, a product of the Romantic cult of
originality. But this is inexact. The ancients had
a concept of plagiarism, though it was not identical to ours. The Latin word *plagiarius,* from
which the English *plagiarist* derives, was first used
(in a surviving document—the actual first use

49

may have been much earlier) in something like its modern sense by the Roman poet Martial in the first century A.D. A *plagiarius* was someone who either stole someone else's slave or enslaved a free person. In his epigram number 52, Martial applied the term metaphorically to another poet, whom Martial accused of having claimed authorship of verses that Martial had written. It is unclear, however, whether he meant that the other poet had passed off Martial's verses as his own or had claimed *sole* ownership (the verses were his slaves), precluding Martial's claiming authorship. Much clearer is epigram number 53, which applies not the word *plagiarius* but the word for thief *(fur)* to someone we would call a plagiarist. The Roman concept of plagiarism or literary theft seems, however, to have been limited to word-for-word copying with no pretense of creativity. Hence the extraordinary Roman genre (originally Greek) of the *cento*—a poem made up entirely of phrases from other poets' poems, rearranged to yield a meaning different from that of any of the originals. That was not considered plagiarism.

The earliest complaints in England about what was soon being called "plagiarism" (the word became common in the seventeenth century) date from Shakespeare's time. Early in his career he himself may have been accused of plagiarism by Robert Greene, though if so (an unresolved issue) the accusation did not stick. Yet was not Shakespeare a plagiarist by modern standards? Thousands of lines in his plays are verbatim copies or close paraphrases from various sources, along with titles and plot details, all without acknowledgment. Most members of his audiences would not have been aware of his appropriations from other writers.

A splendid example of Shakespearean "plagiarism" is the description in *Antony and Cleopatra* of Cleopatra on her barge. This is a blank-verse paraphrase, without acknowledgment, of the description in Sir Thomas North's translation of Plutarch's life of Marc Antony. Here is North:

She disdained to set forward otherwise, but to take her barge in the river of Cydnus; the poope whereof was of gold, the sailes of purple, and the owers [oars] of silver, which kept stroke in rowing after the sounde of the musick of flutes, howboyes, cithens, violls, and such other instruments as they played upon in the barge. And now for the person of her selfe: she was layed under a pavilion of cloth of gold of tissue, apparelled and attired like the goddesse Venus, commonly drawen in picture: and hard by her, on either hand of her, pretie faire boyes apparelled as painters doe set forth god Cupide, with litle fannes in their hands, with the which they fanned wind upon her.

And here Shakespeare:

The barge she sat in, like a burnished throne,
Burnt on the water. The poop was beaten
    gold;

Purple the sails, and so perfumèd that
The winds were lovesick with them. The
　　oars were silver,
Which to the tune of flutes kept stroke, and
　　made
The water which they beat to follow faster,
As amorous of their strokes. For her own
　　person,
It beggared all description: she did lie
In her pavilion—cloth-of-gold of tissue—
O'erpicturing that Venus where we see
The fancy outwork nature. On each side her
Stood pretty dimpled boys, like smiling
　　Cupids,
With divers-colored fans, whose wind did
　　seem
To glow the delicate cheeks which they
　　did cool,
And what they undid did.

If this is plagiarism, we need more plagiarism.
The standard reason given for why it is not pla-

giarism is that in Shakespeare's time, unlike ours, creativity was understood to be improvement rather than originality—in other words, creative imitation. Milton said that "borrowing" from another author, only "if it be not bettered by the borrower, among good authors is accounted Plagiarè." Harold Ogden White refers to "the classical doctrine that true originality is achieved through an imitation which selects its models carefully, reinterprets them personally, and endeavors to surpass them gloriously." The creative imitator sounded variations on an existing theme that he did not attempt to disguise; anyone who knew his Plutarch (though this was not everyone) would have recognized it in the barge scene in *Antony and Cleopatra*.

It is not true, however, that creative imitation is no longer an approved form of creativity and its practitioners are all considered plagiarists. *Tristram Shandy*, written a century and a half after Shakespeare, by which time modern notions of plagiarism were emerging, copies extensively from Robert Burton's *Anatomy of Melancholy* without acknowledgment. Few of Sterne's readers would have recognized the "theft," yet *Tristram Shandy* is a novel of great distinction.

One of the supreme works of twentieth-century literature, T. S. Eliot's long poem "The Waste Land," is a tissue of quotations (without quotation marks) from earlier literature, only imperfectly acknowledged in the notes that Eliot appended to the poem—and among his "borrowings" (he would say "thefts") is the opening of the barge scene from Plutarch North Shakespeare:

> The Chair she sat in, like a burnished
>   throne,
> Glowed on the marble, where the glass
> Held up by standards wrought with
>   fruited vines
> From which a golden Cupidon peeped out
> (Another hid his eyes behind his wing)
> Doubled the flames of sevenbranched
>   candelabra

Reflecting light upon the table as
The glitter of her jewels rose to meet it.

Such appropriations (allusions, as far as the learned reader are concerned—and allusion is a technique of creative imitation) are common in modern poetry. As Eliot explained in an essay on the Jacobean playwright Philip Massinger that describes Eliot's own practice in "The Waste Land" and elsewhere,

> Immature poets imitate; mature poets steal; bad poets deface what they take, and good poets make it into something better, or at least something different. The good poet welds his theft into a whole of feeling which is unique, utterly different from that from which it was torn; the bad poet throws it into something which has no cohesion. A good poet will usually borrow from authors remote in time, or alien in language, or diverse in interest.

Eliot's poetry is heavily indebted to poets like Browning, whom Eliot disparaged, in favor of classical and metaphysical poets, whom he acknowledged as influences, thus throwing the reader off the scent.

Examples are of course not limited to literature. Classical musicians "plagiarize" folk melodies (think of Dvorak, Bartók, and Copland) and often "quote" (as musicians say) from earlier classical works, without being accused of plagiarism. Musical variations on themes of earlier composers further illustrate creative imitation, though there is often acknowledgment in the title (for example, Brahms's "Variations on a Theme by Haydn"). Rap artists "sample" (that is, quote) snatches of earlier songs without explicit acknowledgment, though most rap fans will recognize the quotation.

Édouard Manet's most famous painting, *Déjeuner sur l'Herbe*, contains unmistakable copying of earlier paintings by Raphael, Titian, and Courbet, again without being considered plagiaristic, though only experts would recognize the copy-ings as allusions. (His second most famous paint-ing, *Olympia,* recasts Titian's *Venus d'Urbino* as a French prostitute.) And think of "appropriation art," such as Jeff Koons's sculptural rendition of a photograph (not by him) of a couple cradling eight puppies. The sculpture, which Koons titled *String of Puppies,* looks almost identical to the photograph, although it is much larger, and three-dimensional, of course, and the puppies are col-ored blue.

Here is another example, from Landes's and my book on intellectual property:

The Russian painter George Pusenkoff included in one of his paintings the outline of a nude from a Helmut Newton photo-graph, a distinctive bright blue background from an Yves Klein monochromatic painting, and a small yellow square from a paint-ing by the late Russian artist Casimir Male-vich. Neither Klein nor Malevich's estate objected to Pusenkoff's borrowing, but Newton did and sought to have the painting destroyed. Pusenkoff's defense was that he had created a unique work rather than made multiple copies, that he had borrowed only the outline of a photograph and not the entire photograph, and that he had transformed the photograph by adding public domain material and altering the medium. Yet he clearly had copied Newton's well-known image without paying for it and indeed his stated purpose was to copy recognizable elements from other artists—"to make canvases buzz with cultural associations by 'quoting' from other artists—a perfectly respectable post-modernist approach to picture-making."

Classics are constantly being reworked in new media—such as the novel *Emma* as the movie *Clueless*, or the play *Pygmalion* (itself derived, though very loosely, from Ovid's tale of Pyg-

malion and Galatea) as the musical *My Fair Lady,*
or, similarly, Voltaire's *Candide* as Leonard Bern-
stein's musical *Candide,* or *Romeo and Juliet* as *West
Side Story*—without a sense that plagiarism is
being committed, even though much of the audience for the new work will be ignorant of the
copying. However, if the original is still in copyright, the derivative work, to avoid infringing,
must be licensed by the copyright holder.

In many cases, pretty much the whole audience is expected to recognize the "quotations"
(without quotation marks or other acknowledgment). But that is not critical. In none is the
copying "slavish" rather than creative. These are
regarded as cases of allusion, even if most of the
audience is unaware of the source, rather than of
plagiarism.

To the extent that an imitator or copier produces something better than the original (Shakespeare in his barge scene) or interestingly different
from it (Eliot in his barge scene, or Manet in his
redoing of Titian, among many other examples),
the imitation is producing value. And when, as

is often the case, the person whose work is copied is long dead and the work out of copyright, the copying does not harm him. There is rarely any fraud, moreover, for either the readership or other audience is not fooled by the failure of explicit acknowledgment or it doesn't care about provenance. Koons's sculpture may, as the court said in the suit by the photographer for copyright infringement *(Rogers v. Koons),* have been a species of "piracy" in the sense of a copyright infringement (though probably not, for copying for purposes of parody is generally regarded as fair use), but it was not plagiarism. The satirical intent of the sculpture, prepared for an exhibition called The Banality Show, depended on the audience's realizing that the work was a copy of a sentimental photo rather than an expression of Koons's own taste. And while probably only a handful of the people who saw the movie *Clueless* realized that it was a takeoff on a novel by Jane Austen, the others would not have thought less of the movie (or more of Jane Austen) had they known.

In Shakespeare's case still another factor was at

work—the sheer impracticability of his publicly acknowledging his sources. His plays were not published until after his death, so an acknowledgment in the published texts of copying would not have reached his audiences. And it would have been awkward for one of the actors to have come on stage at the beginning of the play to read a list of the lines that the playwright had copied from other writers. Or consider the following "plagiarism" of Dryden by Pope. Dryden: "For truth has such a face and such a mien / As to be loved needs only to be seen." Pope: "Vice is a monster of so frightful mien / As to be hated needs but to be seen." Should Pope have dropped a footnote acknowledging his close paraphrase of Dryden's couplet? Or listed all such paraphrases in an introduction? That would have been as unnecessary as it would have been awkward, for what was the harm?

The "awkwardness of acknowledgment" may be a reason why it is not considered plagiarism for authors to use a copied phrase as a title: *The*

Sun Also Rises, The Sound and the Fury, For Whom the Bell Tolls, and so on. Many readers will not recognize the allusion, but it would rather spoil the mood that the author is trying to create if he had to note on the title page that his title was a quotation. Furthermore, when as in the examples I gave the quoted phrase is familiar to most readers, they might feel patronized by acknowledgment of the source. And the phrase is being used for a purpose so different from that of its author that we credit the titler with original thinking in picking the passage for his title. All three titles that I mentioned are brilliant, and the brilliance is the titler's as well as the original writer's. In contrast, although titles cannot be copyrighted, an author who uses someone else's title (more commonly, the cleverest part of the title) on his own book is considered fatally lacking in originality—yet is not usually considered a plagiarist, because the title thus copied is invariably that of a well-known book, so there is no deceit.

The awkwardness of acknowledgment extends

beyond plagiarism proper to other cases of failing to give credit for a contribution to a literary or other intellectual work. Important modern examples are Ezra Pound's heavy editing of "The Waste Land," which vastly improved it, and Maxwell Perkins's heavy editing of Thomas Wolfe's novels, which greatly improved them. Should Eliot and Wolfe have acknowledged how large a contribution Pound and Perkins, respectively, had made to their work? Is that information that readers do or should care about? Wouldn't readers prefer to think—this may be a legacy of the Romantic cult of individual genius—that great works of literature spring full grown from the forehead of the named author? Must we disillusion these readers?

The usual sorts of self-plagiarism are further instances of creative imitation. A scholar or other writer who wants to put a new idea across must repeat it, with variations in expression designed to make it more intelligible and palatable to new audiences, and with further variations as he refines the idea and as additional evidence for it accumulates.

The puzzle is not that creative imitation was cherished in Shakespeare's time, as it is today, but that "originality" in the modern sense, in which the imitative element is minimized or at least effectively disguised, was not. Shakespeare could have "made up" his plays rather than, as he invariably did, working from earlier versions or historical materials. One reason he did not may have been that the Elizabethan theater was censored, and this may have inclined playwrights to play it safe by working from plots and themes found in earlier work. Censorship, moreover, reflected a fear of intellectual novelties that was natural in an authoritarian society. And when the market for expressive goods was small and poor, copying provided a means of disseminating work that might otherwise have been inaccessible to most readers. The plagiarist (as we would think him if he were doing the same thing today) was therefore providing a valuable service and so was less likely to be criticized than in our age of cheap copying.

Most important, before cheap books, records, and television, before near-universal literacy and high levels of education and affluence, and before the rise of individualism encouraged people to think for themselves (and thus before the abandonment of censorship and rote learning) and cultivate an individual taste, people's demand for expressive works could be satisfied by a relative handful of works that kept getting improved or elaborated. The cult of originality in its modern sense may thus be largely a consequence of changes in the market for expressive works.

Lisa Pon describes the unfolding of this process in the visual arts during the Italian Renaissance. At first the maker of a print from an artist's drawing was considered the artist's equal; prints were very difficult to make, and they made a work of art available to people who otherwise could not have seen it. As the technology of printmaking improved—as prints became more of a mass-market commodity—the printmaker's contribution to the work of art was devalued. It was devalued not only because less skill was now required to make acceptable prints (that is, more accurate copies of the original drawing) but also because the increased size of the market for the artist's work made him more of a celebrity, a "name," whose prestige was enhanced by his being regarded as the sole creator, even of the prints of his work that were made by others.

The economic story that I am telling may not be the entire explanation for the rise in the value ascribed to originality. Individualism and a cult of originality go hand in hand, and individualism is characteristic of modernity. As society grows more complex, creating more differentiated roles for its members to play, and as the spread of education and prosperity frees people from the shackles of custom, family, and authority and encourages each person to be an individual, a "cult of personality" emerges. Each of us thinks that our contribution to society is unique and so deserves public recognition, which plagiarism clouds. Individualism also creates heterogeneity of demands for expressive and intellectual products, as of physical products and ordinary commercial services; and the greater the demand for variety—for many new things rather than for incremental improvements in the old—the greater the demand for originality.

When the market for expressive goods was thin, moreover, writers and artists depended heavily on patronage to finance their work—consumers weren't numerous or affluent enough to do so. An author who has a patron is less likely to worry about competition than one who lives and dies by his ability to satisfy a market of anonymous buyers who have competitive alternatives. As the market for expressive works expanded, the method of financing them shifted from patronage to sales. Because the new financiers of intellectual goods—the consumers—unlike the patrons did not know the author personally, it became important that he be identified by name so that consumers' experience with one of his books could guide their decision on whether to buy other of his books.

One can chart the rise of the market for expressive works by tracing the decline of anonymous authorship. Naming the author, like naming a manufacturer, establishes a brand identity in order to attract consumers, and by the same token invites fraud because an author may be able to enhance his "brand" in the eyes of consumers by copying the work of competitors or of predecessors without acknowledgment. The resemblance of plagiarism to trademark infringement—to passing off one's inferior brand as a well-known superior brand (remember Rembrandt)—is not an accident. Trademark infringement in the market for ordinary goods corresponds to plagiarism in the market for expressive goods. Trademarks and author "branding" (by naming) coevolved as ways of protecting sellers and consumers as markets expanded and became impersonal.

The larger the body of expressive works, moreover, the easier it is to commit fraud because of the infeasibility of exhaustive search, though this problem may be on the way to solution by the development of plagiarism-detection software.

So the economics of modernity can tell us much about the changing meaning and significance of plagiarism. It can tell us, for example, why Kaavya Viswanathan's copying of a passage from a novel by Megan McCafferty is not excusable as creative imitation. A glance back at the two passages will reveal that Viswanathan made changes that improved on McCafferty (although the wit is McCafferty's). And probably most of Viswanathan's book is original. In the seventeenth century she might have escaped condemnation as a plagiarist. What might have been deemed creative imitation then is unequivocally plagiarism today. What has changed? One thing that has changed is that a seventeenth-century counterpart to McCafferty would have been unlikely to derive significant income from writing. Most likely she would have written for private circulation or for a patron. Had someone received a copy of one of her works and touched it up and circulated it as her own, the harm to her pocketbook would have been slight or nonexistent. All is changed. Viswanathan was poised to become a major competitor of McCafferty for the "chick-lit" market. Had her plagiarism not been quickly detected, she might have made significant inroads into McCafferty's market—in part by using McCafferty's own words against her, as it were. Creative imitation cannot have as capacious a scope or as positive a connotation in a modern commercial society of commodified intellectual works as it did in Shakespeare's time.

We can better understand and extenuate Shakespeare's practice of copying by asking why any writer of works intended to entertain would *want* to be "original." He would want to make the best work he could according to the intended audience's judgment. This might require him to copy large stretches of other people's writings into his work—which would also enable him to save time, and thus to produce more works. (This remains the situation and outlook of judges, and is why "judicial plagiarism" is an oxymoron.) Readers are no more interested in originality as such than eaters are. They are interested in the quality of the reading experience that a work gives them. Originality becomes important only when the reading market is so dense that readers become jaded and therefore require variety to keep them entertained. There weren't hundreds of thousands of books in print or in libraries in Shakespeare's time; the plays of his predecessors were not available on DVDs. If he wrote a new *Romeo and Juliet* there was little danger that the audience would complain that he was stealing from Arthur Brooke, who had written a narrative poem called *Romeus and Juliet* several decades earlier, or that both Brooke and Shakespeare had taken the story of Romeo and Juliet from Ovid's tale of Pyramus and Thisbe (a story also "stolen" directly by Shakespeare—it is the play within a play in *A Midsummer Night's Dream*). The demand for originality is an economic phenomenon anchored in time and place. Just what "originality" means, however, remains to be considered.

As we saw earlier, there is still plenty of creative imitation. There might be still more were it not for the rise of copyright. (Might, not would, because without copyright protection there might be fewer books written and therefore less to copy.) The effect of copyright is to place most creative imitation of copyrighted works at the sufferance of the owners of the copyrights on those works. Had there been copyright in Shakespeare's day, his close copying of other writers' plots would have marked him as an infringer. The imitator remains free as a matter of copyright law to plunder the public domain, consisting of works no longer (some of them never were) protected by copyright. But it is possible that by limiting the scope for free creative imitation, copyright has encouraged rather than simply mirrored a growing belief that literary, artistic, and other intellectual goods are not really "creative" unless they are "original." That belief rests on the absurd idea that "copying" is inherently bad (so "copycat" is a pejorative, though the activity from which the word is derived—the close imitation by kittens of their mother's behavior—is obviously not a case of plagiarism). But it has influenced the modern meaning of plagiarism.

V

OURS IS A TIME and place in which market forces favor originality and in which a robust concept of plagiarism backs up the market valuation. But how *grave* is the problem of plagiarism today? This depends in part on the breadth of the concept, which must not be exaggerated. Creative imitation, though more narrowly conceived than in Shakespeare's day, is not plagiarism. Nor is self-plagiarism, other than in exceptional cases. And caution must be the watchword when the concept of plagiarism is extended from literal copying to the copying of ideas. Another term for copying an idea, as distinct from copying the specific form of words or sounds or images in which it is expressed, is disseminating an idea. If one needs a license to repeat another person's idea, or if one risks ostracism by one's professional community for failing to credit an idea to its originator, who may be forgotten or unknown, the dissemination of ideas is impeded.

We should also be wary of "plagiarism denouncing" as a device of professional self-promotion. Journalists have a bad reputation for accuracy; and historians in our postmodernist era are suspected of having embraced an extreme form of relativism and of having lost their regard for facts. (We shall see that some postmodernists do indeed question the concept of plagiarism.) Both professions hope by taking a hard line against plagiarism and fabrication to reassure the public that their practitioners are serious diggers after truth whose efforts, a form of "sweat equity," deserve protection against copycats.

There is also a crowding phenomenon that would make plagiarism, if defined too broadly, unavoidable. The desire to be original and the desire to be successful are not wholly compatible. Publishers are not looking for works to publish that are completely original, because they can have no idea how the reading public will respond; in fact avant garde work does not achieve commercial success until it has ceased to be in advance of popular taste. Publishers are looking for the new thing that's enough like the old thing to be likely to gain early acceptance by the market, yet enough unlike it to satisfy the public's taste for variety. The creation of such works would be stymied by equating imitation to plagiarism. Creative imitation is not just a classical or Renaissance legacy; it is a modern market imperative.

The need to walk a fine line is even more acute in the movie industry, because the typical studio makes only a few movies a year, each of which may be enormously expensive. The risk and cost of failure are both very great; hence the extraordinary degree to which new movies are based on books, plays, and, especially, earlier movies that have proved to be commercial successes, hence, too, the remaking of the same movie *(The Twenty-Nine Steps, King Kong, Henry V)*, the endless sequels, and the incessant repetition of successful formulas.

We should also be careful not to confuse innocent forms of copying with plagiarism, but at the same time not to equate innocent to unintentional. Negligent copying can do the same harm as deliberate. Law has a concept of negligent as well as of intentional misrepresentation, and imposes liability for both. Law also has a concept of unavoidable accidents, for which generally there is no liability. But there is no copying so extensive as to trigger serious charges of plagiarism that the copier could not have avoided by taking reasonable care. Plagiarism can be deliberate or negligent, but at least when it is extensive, it is never unavoidable.

The distinction between deliberate and negligent plagiarism bears on the proper punishment. Some types of plagiarism merit ostracism, ridicule, and cancellation of contracts, others lesser sanctions. Legal analogies are again helpful. In deciding how severely to punish a crime, legislators and judges consider the harm it does but also the incentive to commit it. That depends in part on the ease or difficulty of detection. The more difficult the criminal's deed is to detect, and the easier, therefore, it is for him to get away with his crime, the greater his incentive to commit the crime; and the greater that incentive is, the more severe the punishment must be in order to deter its commission.

Weak students and also very ambitious ones have a strong incentive to plagiarize if they have a good chance of getting away with it and the punishment if they are caught is not too severe. In contrast, plagiarism in a published work is impossible to conceal in the usual case in which the work plagiarized was also published. (The usual case, but not the only one. Recall Professor Kirshner's plagiarism. Since the student who was the victim of the plagiarism was the only person in a position to detect it, had he not blown the whistle the plagiarism would not have been detected.) That is not the only reason to expect plagiarism to be committed less frequently by teachers than by students. Another is that fewer scholars are as strongly motivated to plagiarize as students are. Scholars are self-selected into an activity that requires them to write, although not to write well (which means, however, that good writing is not highly valued in most scholarly fields). They are not indifferent students with writer's block.

A deterrent to plagiarism by popular writers is that the greater the commercial success of the plagiarizing work, the more certain its plagiarisms are to be detected. So success becomes a double-edged sword. Kaavya Viswanathan's plagiarism was certain to be detected because *Opal Mehta* was aimed at the same readership as Megan McCafferty's books. Even if ordinary readers didn't notice the plagiarism, McCafferty and her publisher were bound to discover it because they would be sure to read with care a work by a new, potentially formidable competitor. Another certainty was that Viswanathan's youth and Harvard connection and the size of her advance would draw intense media scrutiny if her plagiarism was discovered. It would be the modern equivalent of placing a criminal in stocks at the side of a very busy thoroughfare.

Given the certainty of detection, one might think that Viswanathan was punished too severely by the avalanche of negative publicity that, sure enough, descended on her when her plagiarism was discovered. But one reason for the amount of that publicity was her audacity—her sheer recklessness—in committing a "crime" for which she was sure to be caught. She fascinated the public with the spectacle of her dizzying overreaching—the height of her rise and the suddenness and depth of her fall. But more than spectacle was involved. A mild punishment would be unlikely to deter a person who had such a compulsion to plagiarize regardless of the foreseeable consequences; even a threat of severe punishment had not deterred Viswanathan.

Student plagiarism may be becoming less common as more and more colleges and universities adopt plagiarism-detection software, such as Turnitin, a product of a company named iParadigms. Thousands of colleges both in the United States and abroad have acquired licenses, at an annual cost of about 80 cents per enrolled student, to use the program. The program digitizes each student's paper, uploads it into the Turnitin database, and searches the database for matches. The Turnitin database is actually a collection of databases. One, the equivalent of Google's database, is a complete and continuously updated copy of the World Wide Web. Others contain archived materials from the Web, contents of other publicly available databases—and all the student papers that have been submitted to Turnitin for a plagiarism check.

Some especially tony colleges, such as Harvard, do not subscribe to Turnitin or other plagiarism-detection software services but prefer to preach to their students about the evils of plagiarism. These schools are naïve. True, their students are abler on average than the students at lesser colleges. But no college has a uniformly able and motivated student body, when one considers athletic scholarships, legacy admissions, and affirmative action. Abler students tend also to be more ambitious than mediocre ones, and ambition can be a tempter. What is true, however, is that a clever teacher can make it difficult for his students to plagiarize simply by the nature of the assignments he gives. If, for example, he assigns his students to write essays comparing two disparate writers, philosophers, etc. (Homer and Tom Clancy, Gibbon and Doris Kearns Goodwin), they will not be able to find a previously published comparison. But there will be pedagogical distortion, as my examples are intended to suggest.

Turnitin's home page explains that "every paper submitted [for a plagiarism check] is returned [to the customer] in the form of a customized Originality Report. Results are based on exhaustive searches of billions of pages from both current and archived instances of the Internet, millions of student papers previously submitted to Turnitin, and commercial databases of journal articles and periodicals." The report contains an "Overall Similarity Index," but the customer decides whether the amount of unacknowledged copying reported constitutes plagiarism warranting discipline.

It might seem that a Turnitin search would return too many false positives to be useful, since very short strings of common words appear in many different documents without having been copied (for example, "on the next day"). But Turnitin does not "alert" to possible plagiarism unless the match is of strings long enough to be unlikely to have been hit on independently by two or more writers. Once such an identical passage is found, however, the program will search for shorter strings in the vicinity of the trigger passage. So the plagiarist can't thwart the program merely by changing a few words. There will be some false positives, because of indented quotations, which do not bear quotation marks;

and some false negatives—Viswanathan's plagiarism from McCafferty that I quoted was flagrant, but because Viswanathan made frequent, albeit minor, changes, the identical strings were very short.

Turnitin might seem incapable of catching students who plagiarize copyrighted books, since few such books are as yet in publicly available electronic databases. But quotations from books can often be found on the Web (in online book reviews, for example), or in previously submitted student papers retained in the Turnitin database, and if those quotations appear without quotation marks in the paper undergoing a Turnitin search, the plagiarism will be detected.

Programs such as Turnitin are only a few years old. Apparently they are as yet little used by publishers to protect themselves from what befell Little, Brown as a result of Viswanathan's plagiarism. Maybe some publishers would prefer not to find out that they're publishing a plagiarist. The plagiarism may improve the book and not be discovered until the book is out of print. Damages from copyright infringement may be difficult to prove, but if the publisher *knew* he was infringing he would face criminal penalties; better, then, not to know. But given the heavy blow that Little, Brown sustained in the Viswanathan affair, it may be only a matter of time before most publishers begin using Turnitin or similar programs. We may be entering the twilight of plagiarism.

Among the less serious forms of plagiarism is the copying, by popular writers, of work that is not aimed at or valued by the popular market, provided there is at least a general acknowledgment of the copying, as distinct from quotation marks and footnoted references. Suppose a popular historian copies passages from a scholarly article by an academic historian who has no aspiration to publish popular history, and the copying improves the popular history. The popular historian will probably touch up the copied passages to make them fit more smoothly into his narrative; and this will preclude the use of quotation marks. Even if the copying is literal, the copier will want to avoid quotation marks if only because from the reader's standpoint they are merely a distraction. The author of the copied work would not be harmed—on the contrary, the (acknowledged—that is important) copying would get him some favorable publicity, and the readership of his work would be increased by its being copied in a popular work.

This would be an example of creative imitation. And since a popular historian does not claim to be an original discoverer or interpreter of historical events, his appropriations of the original work of others would not give him a reputation for originality that he could trade on. It is different if a student copies without acknowledgment, or a professor, or a journalist. For they are judged by their originality, whether in the form of a new idea or a distinctive mode of expression or, in the case of the journalist, and of many scientists and historians, the discovery of a previously unknown fact or the development of a new insight.

So suppose Doris Kearns Goodwin had said in

the preface to her book on the Kennedys: "I am going to quote extensively from Lynne McTaggart, the author of a previous book, but I'm not going to put my quotations in quotation marks as that would interrupt the narrative flow and distract the reader." This revelation would be a confession of copyright infringement unless McTaggart's work was out of copyright or she had given Goodwin permission to copy. But I would hesitate to call it plagiarism. (Goodwin did footnote her references to McTaggart's work, but footnotes acknowledge the sources of ideas; they do not acknowledge copying the source's words.)

VI

WHAT DRIVES PEOPLE to plagiarize and what drives the public responses to plagiarism, whether punitive or extenuating? The answers are straightforward with respect to plagiarism by students. They plagiarize to save time, to get better grades, or both; the effect on learning and evaluation is significant and punishment often and appropriately severe. Plagiarism by professors tends to be punished less severely, as in Kirshner's case (also Tribe's and Ogletree's). This is not only because plagiarism in published work is more likely to be detected than plagiarism in an unpublished student paper (and remember that the more detectable an offense, the lighter the punishment that will deter its commission, though not in every case)—for that was not Kirshner's case. It is also because professors identify more with other professors than with students ("there but for the grace of God go I")—we judge less harshly those malefactors who are most like us and with whom we can therefore empathize most easily. The resulting double standard outrages students and breeds warranted cynicism toward academics' pretensions of adhering to a moral standard higher than that of the commercial marketplace. But it is also worth noting that the student who plagiarizes produces nothing of value, whereas a professor who appropriates ideas or even phrases and incorporates them into his own work produces a better product. Yet this effect (missing by the way in Kirshner's case) is outweighed by the fact that professorial plagiarism gives students negative role models, and by the greater capacity for moral reflection that we presume of older persons.

There is also, however, a sense that plagiarism by a published writer is a chump's crime, less likely to reflect a serious larcenous intent than a loose screw. The more successful the writer, the more nutty-seeming the plagiarism. Doris Kearns Goodwin is an able writer, and it seems unlikely that the success of her book on the Kennedy family was due to any great extent to her plagiarisms. The case of another popular historian, Stephen Ambrose, is more complex. His plagiarisms were very extensive and may have enabled him to write more books than he could otherwise have done. (Kaavya Viswanathan's plagiarisms were so extensive that it is unclear whether her book would have had good prospects without them.) Yet both Goodwin's and especially Ambrose's books were so widely read that their plagiarisms were bound to be detected. In both cases discovery came later rather than sooner, yet the gains that an author can reasonably expect from plagiarizing are usually smaller than the expected costs in disgrace (the costs, if the plagiarism is discovered, discounted by the probability that it will be discovered). Even Goodwin will long bear the scars of her plagiarism. The net gains from plagiarism are further reduced by the fact that generous acknowledgment, the use of quotation marks, and perhaps even careful paraphrasing will get the would-be plagiarist off the hook without his losing most of the benefit of his copying or having to shoulder a heavy burden of rewriting.

The seemingly gratuitous character of the offense when committed by professional writers is part of the reason there seem always to be people willing to leap to the defense of the detected plagiarist. Viswanathan, caught before she had a body of distinguished work, has few extenuators; Goodwin, Ambrose, the radical historian Philip Foner, Martin Luther King Jr., and other notable plagiarists have many.

Goodwin left nothing to chance. She hired the political consultant Robert Shrum to drum up support for her in the media. Laurence Tribe leapt quickly to her defense, contending that her plagiarism had been inadvertent (though there was no way he could have determined that to be the case)—like his! And a string of prominent historians led by Arthur Schlesinger Jr. signed an open letter to the *New York Times* stating flatly that Goodwin "did not, she does not, cheat or plagiarize. In fact, her character and work symbolize the highest standards of moral integrity." Yet Goodwin had acknowledged "inadvertent" copying from the works of several authors, claiming implausibly to have forgotten having written out in longhand verbatim passages from those works and to have thought them her own notes—as if there were no stylistic differences between her writing and that of other writers. Moreover, when "outed" she had failed to acknowledge the extent of the copying; had failed also to acknowledge having paid an undisclosed amount of money in a legal settlement, presumably for copyright infringement, with Lynne McTaggart.

It is remarkable that professional historians, usually so quick to denounce plagiarism, should declare an acknowledged plagiarist to be a moral exemplar because her plagiarisms *may* (improbably) have been inadvertent. They must have forgotten the American Historical Association's admonition, which might have been written with Goodwin in mind, that "the plagiarist's standard defense—that he or she was misled by hastily taken and imperfect notes—is plausible only in the context of a wider tolerance of shoddy work."

Politics may have played the decisive role in Goodwin's surprisingly swift rehabilitation, as we'll see; and, speaking of politics, I note that one reason for the ambivalence of reactions to plagiarism is that the Left, which dominates intellectual circles in the United States, is soft on plagiarism. Notions of genius, of individual creativity, and of authorial celebrity, which inform the condemnation of plagiarism, make the leftist uncomfortable because they seem to celebrate inequality and "possessive individualism" (that is, capitalism). Debora Halbert asserts that "for the feminist and the postmodernist, appropriation or plagiarism are [sic] acts of sedition against an already established mode of knowing, a way of knowing indebted to male creation and property rights." And Rebecca Moore Howard—a practitioner of "liberatory pedagogy"—believes that students should not be punished for what she calls "patchwriting" and defines as "copying from a source text and then deleting some words, altering grammatical structures, or plugging in one synonym for another." Viswanathan's copying from McCafferty fits Howard's definition of "patchwriting" to a T.

Intellectuals of all political persuasions tend to mock the application of notions of originality and creativity to modern American culture. Are McCafferty's "chick-lit" novels so worthy an achievement that a copier should be anathematized? But the norm against plagiarism no more depends on cultural distinction than the norm against trademark infringement does. What Viswanathan did was no less—though maybe no more—reprehensible than what a manufacturer of toothpaste would be doing if he slapped the name of a better-known brand on his toothpaste, even if his toothpaste was equal in quality to that of the other brand.

We need to distinguish between "originality" and "creativity," stripping the former of the normative overtones that rightly attend the latter. An original work is simply something that is different enough from some existing work that it could not be confused with it. From an aesthetic standpoint the work might not have been worth making. It might be unimaginative hack work. But in a commercial society anything that fills an empty niche, however tiny, in market space has value, and that value is diminished by plagiarism. If "originality" as used in Turnitin's Originality Reports were equated to creativity, very few student papers would be original, yet obviously not all unoriginal student papers are plagiaristic. A publisher's reprinting a book under the author's name is an acknowledged copying, so it is not plagiarism despite being wholly unoriginal.

The other side of this coin is that acknowledgment, while it negates any charge of plagiarism (though not of copyright infringement), does not establish originality. To say that someone is not a plagiarist is a feeble compliment.

Unconscious plagiarism is a sin of neglect rather than of intention and, therefore, less blameworthy, so when plagiarists are caught they invariably argue that their plagiarism was unconscious. Viswanathan pushed this excuse aggressively. There is even a word for unconscious plagiarism—*cryptomnesia*. The plagiarist had read something and he remembers it without remembering that he had read it. Psychologists have investigated the phenomenon and have found no evidence that people can recite entire passages written by someone else yet believe they are their own—no evidence of a photographic memory that forgets the act of photographing.

The excuse of innocent plagiarism of verbal passages of more than trivial length is plausible only in the case of a book acknowledged to be a "managed" book: the nominal author, really an editor, has assembled the writings of others whom he hired for the purpose, such as his student research assistants. If *they* plagiarized, he may be unable to detect the plagiarism. The "managed" book may seem quintessentially a work of plagiarism even if the writers are scrupulous. But it is not if its character is acknowledged by the "manager" or is otherwise known to its readers, as apparently was not the case, however, with Ogletree's book. Many legal treatises and elementary and high school textbooks are managed books, but not all, so it would be a service to readers if the managers disclosed their true role, which they do not do.

Peter Paul Rubens managed a large staff that did the actual painting of many of his works, though under his supervision. Some successful artists of his era (and earlier) used assistants to create paintings from the artist's drawings or to paint hands or other secondary features in the master's paintings. The assistants did not sign the paintings; only the master did. But there was no plagiarism so long as the buyers of the paintings were aware of the practice.

Unconscious plagiarism is a more plausible defense to a charge of copying someone's idea or tune, as distinct from his words, without attribution. It is common enough to remember an idea or a short run of musical notes without remembering its origin—and if it is an idea in your field, or you are a musician, you may think that the idea or the tune, as the case may be, is original with you. And because ideas do not have the fixity of sentences, it is often unclear whether a new idea is so like an old one that it should be classified as a copy. There is an analogy to paraphrase, which at some point ceases to be a copy. But you can compare the paraphrase to the original word for word to see how close it is to the original, and you cannot do that with ideas, because they can be expressed in different words. Indeed at some level of generality there are no new ideas. Democritus invented atomic theory before the birth of Christ, and Aristarchus of

Samos discovered that the earth revolves around the sun more than a thousand years before Copernicus, who gets all the credit, rediscovered it. Psychological studies of cryptomnesia find that people who improve on or otherwise elaborate other people's ideas come to think of the ideas as having originated with themselves.

The most important distinction between plagiarism of verbal passages, musical motifs, and paintings, on the one hand, and plagiarism of ideas, on the other—a distinction that suggests that much copying of ideas isn't plagiarism at all—is that old ideas are constantly being rediscovered by people unaware that the ideas had been discovered already. Simultaneous discovery or invention (for example of calculus, by Leibniz and Newton, or of evolution, by Darwin and Wallace) is also common. A rediscoverer or independent discoverer is not a copier, hence not a plagiarist. Often, it is true, the rediscoverer can be criticized for not having done thorough enough research to have learned that the ideas he thought original with himself had originated with someone else. Such oversights harm the original discoverer, at least if he is still alive, and if careless could well be thought a form of misconduct. But it is not plagiarism because it is not copying.

Because innocent plagiarism of ideas, and honest rediscovery, are plausible, and the plagiarism itself often uncertain (at what point does the elaborator deserve the real credit?), deliberate plagiarism of ideas is extremely common; for it is easy to get away with just by denying that it was deliberate. Academics regularly exaggerate their originality without being accused of plagiarism. Their exaggerations are excused under the anodyne rubric "anticipated," an equivocation because it is not limited to genuine rediscoveries, which involve no awareness of the original. If research discovers that a distinguished academic's "original" idea had been propounded much earlier, this is said to be a case of anticipation, not of plagiarism. The anticipator is often dismissed as someone who made a lucky guess or who discovered an idea prematurely—that is, before the world was ready or able to use it (as in the case of both Democritus and Aristarchus)—and his contribution is discounted accordingly. Most scholars in a culture that prizes originality give as little credit to their predecessors as they can decently get away with.

Ideas can be plagiarized even in a literary work, and even though "idea" as we saw has usually a different meaning from what it would bear in a work of science or history. A recent book by Michael Maar asks whether Vladimir Nabokov's novel *Lolita* plagiarized a short story of the same name published many years earlier by a German named Heinz von Eschwege, with whom Nabokov overlapped for a number of years in Berlin. No verbal passages are identical, but apart from the story's having the same title as Nabokov's novel, von Eschwege's eponymous heroine like Nabokov's is a nymphet with whom the first-person narrator, an older man like Humbert

Humbert, falls in love. In both tales they meet in a boardinghouse by a body of water (the Mediterranean in von Eschwege's tale, a lake in Nabokov's); in both the girl is the seducer, is accursed, demonic, dies. The femme fatale motif is common enough—is an example of a literary idea that can be copied without plagiarism or copyright infringement—and von Eschwege's Lolita unlike Nabokov's is, though a young girl, not clearly a child. Yet given the identity in the names, pure coincidence seems unlikely.

Maybe Nabokov read the story, or perhaps heard it described, and then forgot it; maybe he remembered but concealed his debt because von Eschwege had become a prominent Nazi journalist; or maybe he feared being accused of plagiarism if he acknowledged his predecessor. It hardly matters. Von Eschwege was dead by the time Nabokov's *Lolita* was published, and if ever there was a case of creative imitation it was Nabokov's elaboration of the germ (von Eschwege's story is only thirteen pages long) of the idea that he may have gotten from the earlier writer. Even if the copying was deliberate, it was not plagiarism, any more than Shakespeare's copyings were plagiarisms, or, to take an apter comparison, Milton's massive elaboration in *Paradise Lost* of the story of the Garden of Eden told in Genesis.

So what then of Pia Pera's *Diario di Lo* (*Lolita's Diary*), an Italian novel published in 1995? An explicit takeoff on *Lolita,* it retells Nabokov's novel but from the standpoint of Lolita herself. About two-thirds of the novel sticks closely to the original, both in plot details and in wording; the rest consists of a narrative of Lolita's life before she met Humbert Humbert and after she left him (for she does not die in *Diario di Lo*). When Nabokov's estate learned that an English edition of *Diario di Lo* was planned, it sued for copyright infringement. (The case was settled out of court.) The book is of course derivative from *Lolita,* but it is not a parody, where greater license in copying is permitted; that is, it is not a critique of *Lolita*. And it is not plagiarism, because it makes no effort to conceal its debts to *Lolita;* indeed it flaunts them. Nor is there any effort to pass off the work as Nabokov's; he died many years before *Diario di Lo* was written, and Pera does not pretend that it is a previously unknown Nabokov manuscript.

In Shakespeare's time, *Diario di Lo* might well have been considered a proper effort at creative imitation. Changing fashions in "originality" condemn such imitations when not authorized by the copyright owner. Flaunting as we know is no defense to copyright infringement, but as always we should avoid conflating plagiarism with infringement.

VII

IT IS TIME to sum up. Plagiarism is a species of intellectual fraud. It consists of unauthorized copying that the copier claims (whether explicitly or implicitly, and whether deliberately or carelessly) is original with him and the claim causes the copier's audience to behave otherwise than it would if it knew the truth. This change in behavior, as when it takes the form of readers' buying the copier's book under the misapprehension that it is original, can harm both the person who is copied and the competitors of the copier. But there can be plagiarism without publication, as in the case of student plagiarism. The fraud is directed in the first instance at the teacher (assuming the student bought rather than stole the paper that he copied). But its principal victims are the plagiarist's student competitors, who are analogous to authors who compete with a plagiarist.

Plagiarism is considered by most writers, teachers, journalists, scholars, and even members of the general public to be the capital intellectual crime. In James Hynes's satirical novella of plagiarism, *Casting the Runes,* the plagiarist, having by black magic murdered one of the historians whom he plagiarized and tried to murder a second, is himself killed by the same black magic, deployed by the widow of his murder victim. Being caught out in plagiarism can blast a politician's career, earn a college student expulsion, and destroy a writer's, scholar's, or journalist's reputation, though whether it has any of these effects depends on a host of extraneous factors. Doris Kearns Goodwin may have escaped with her career more or less intact because she was a prominent liberal outed by a conservative magazine (the *Weekly Standard*) and extravagantly defended by her prominent liberal friends. Charges of plagiarism can thus figure in political battles, as Senator Biden, outed by the campaign manager of his rival presidential aspirant, Michael Dukakis, learned to his sorrow; maybe Goodwin, too, was a political victim, though this should not extenuate her offense.

The subject of plagiarism requires cool appraisal rather than fervid condemnation or simplistic apologetics. The temptation to lump distinct practices in with plagiarism should be resisted for the sake of clarity; "self-plagiarism," for example, should be recognized as a distinct practice and rarely an objectionable one. The vagueness of the concept of plagiarism should be acknowledged and thus a gray area recognized in which creative imitation produces value that should undercut a judgment of plagiarism—indeed an imitator may produce greater value than an originator, once "originality" is understood, as it should be if we are to understand plagiarism in properly relativistic terms, just to mean difference, not necessarily creativity. In modern commercial society, which places the stamp of personality on goods both physical and intellectual for economic reasons unrelated to high culture, a verdict of plagiarism is pronounced without regard to the quality of the plagiarized original or, for that matter, of the plagiarizing copy.

In the course of my cook's tour of the principal issues that have to be addressed in order to form a thoughtful response to plagiarism in modern America, I have challenged its definition as "literary theft" and in its place emphasized reliance, detectability, and the extent of the market for expressive works as keys to defining plagiarism and calibrating the different types of plagiarism by their gravity. I have emphasized the variety of plagiarisms, argued for the adequacy of the existing, informal sanctions, pointed out that the "fair use" doctrine of copyright law should not protect a plagiarist, noted the analogy between plagiarism and trademark infringement (a clue to the entwinement of the modern concept of plagiarism with market values)—and warned would-be plagiarists that the continuing advance of digitization may soon trip them up.

ACKNOWLEDGMENTS AND
BIBLIOGRAPHICAL NOTE

I thank Meghan Maloney for her excellent research assistance, John Barrie for helpful discussion of Turnitin (his company's plagiarism-detection software program), Peter Skilton for information about *Diario di Lo,* and Erroll McDonald, William Patry, Richard Stern, and Beth Vesel for illuminating comments on the manuscript of this book.

The full citations to the secondary works mentioned in the text are as follows:

Banga, Aditi. "Fighting Plagiarism, Schools Go High Tech." *Harvard Crimson,* online edition, May 4, 2006, www.thecrimson.com/article.aspx?ref=513316 (accessed May 24, 2006).

Bloom, Harold. *The Anxiety of Influence: A Theory of Poetry.* 2nd edition. New York: Oxford University Press, 1997.

Crimson Staff. " 'Opal Mehta' Gone for Good; Contract Cancelled." *Harvard Crimson,* online edition, May 2,

2006, www.thecrimson.com/article.aspx?ref=513231
(accessed May 24, 2006).

Eliot, T. S. "Philip Massinger." In Eliot, *The Sacred Wood: Essays on Poetry and Criticism*. London: Methuen; New York: Barnes & Noble, 1960, pp. 123, 125.

Glatzer, Jenna. "Book Packaging: Under-Explored Terrain for Free-lancers." www.absolutewrite.com/site/book_packaging.htm (accessed August 3, 2006).

Halbert, Debora. "Poaching and Plagiarizing: Property, Plagiarism, and Feminist Futures." In *Perspectives on Plagiarism and Intellectual Property in a Postmodern World*, ed. Lise Buranen and Alice M. Roy. Albany: State University of New York Press, 1999, pp. 111, 116.

Howard, Rebecca Moore. *Standing in the Shadow of Giants: Plagiarists, Authors, Collaborators*. Stanford, Conn.: Ablex Publishing, 1999.

Landes, William M., and Richard A. Posner. *The Economic Structure of Intellectual Property Law*. Cambridge, Mass.: Belknap Press, 2003, chap. 9.

Maar, Michael. *The Two Lolitas*. London; New York: Verso, 2005.

Pfister, Bonnie. "Now Infamous U.S. Teen Author Remembered as Principled High School Student." Associated Press, May 11, 2006.

Pon, Lisa. *Raphael, Dürer, and Marcantonio Raimondi: Copying and the Italian Renaissance Print.* New Haven, Conn.: Yale University Press, 2004.

Ricks, Christopher. "Plagiarism." In *Plagiarism in Early Modern England,* ed. Paulina Kewes. New York: Palgrave Macmillan, 2003, p. 21.

Rogers v. Koons, 960 F.2d 301 (2d Cir. 1992).

Schemo, Diana Jean. "Schoolbooks Are Given F's in Originality." *New York Times,* July 13, 2006, p. A1.

"Turnitin." www.turnitin.com/static/home.html (accessed June 16, 2006).

White, Harold Ogden. *Plagiarism and Imitation During the English Renaissance: A Study in Critical Distinctions.* New York: Octagon Books, 1965.

Zhou, David. "Example of Similar Passages Between Viswanathan's Book and McCafferty's Two Novels." *Harvard Crimson,* online edition, April 23, 2006, www.thecrimson.com/article.aspx?ref=512965 (accessed August 3, 2006).

———. "Publisher Pulls 'Opal Mehta.' " *Harvard Crimson,* online edition, April 28, 2006, www.thecrimson.com/article.aspx?ref=513153 (accessed May 24, 2006).

———. "Publisher Rejects Soph's Apology." *Harvard Crimson,* online edition, April 26, 2006, www.thecrimson.com/article.aspx?ref=513041 (accessed May 24, 2006).

And here are references to some other works (some of which discuss charges of plagiarism examined in this book) that the reader may find interesting:

Baruch, Gregory. "Artful Deception: If Ghostwriters Are Indispensable, Why Are They So Invisible?" *Washington Post*, March 31, 2002, p. B1.

Carroll, Marie, and Timothy J. Perfect. "Students' Experience of Unconscious Plagiarism: Did I Beget or Forget?" In *Applied Metacognition*, ed. Timothy J. Perfect and Bennett L. Schwartz. New York: Cambridge University Press, 2002, p. 146.

Clark, Roy Peter. "The Unoriginal Sin." *Washington Journalism Review*, March 1983, p. 43.

Freedman, Morris. "The Persistence of Plagiarism, the Riddle of Originality." *Virginia Quarterly Review* 70, no. 3: 504–18.

Fruman, Norman. *Coleridge, the Damaged Archangel*. New York: George Braziller, 1971.

Green, Stuart P. "Plagiarism, Norms, and the Limits of Theft Law." *Hastings Law Journal* 54, no. 1 (2002–2003): 167–242.

Grossman, Ron. "Petty Plagiarism Is Stain on U[niversity]. of C[hicago]." *Chicago Tribune*, June 16, 1996, p. D3.

History News Network. "How the Goodwin Story Developed." hnn.us/articles/590.html (accessed August 3, 2006).

Lerman, Lisa. "Misattribution in Legal Scholarship: Plagiarism, Ghostwriting, and Authorship." *South Texas Law Review* 42, no. 2 (spring 2001): 467–92.

Lindey, Alexander. *Plagiarism and Originality.* New York: Harper, 1952.

Mallon, Thomas. *Stolen Words.* First Harvest edition. San Diego: Harcourt, 2001.

Mawdsley, Ralph D. "Legal Aspects of Plagiarism." Topeka, Kan.: National Organization on Legal Problems of Education, 1985.

Mnookin, Seth. "The DaVinci Clone?" *Vanity Fair,* July 2006, p. 101.

Orgel, Stephen. "Plagiarism and Original Sin." In *Plagiarism in Early Modern England,* ed. Paulina Kewes. New York: Palgrave Macmillan, 2003, p. 56.

Paull, H. M. *Literary Ethics: A Study in the Growth of the Literary Conscience.* London: T. Butterworth, 1928.

Randall, Marilyn. *Pragmatic Plagiarism: Authorship, Profit, and Power.* Toronto; Buffalo, N.Y.: University of Toronto Press, 2001.

Ruthven, K. K. *Faking Literature.* New York: Cambridge University Press, 2001, chap. 5.

St. Onge, K. R. *The Melancholy Anatomy of Plagiarism.* Lanham, Md.: University Press of America, 1998.

Wiener, Jon. *Historians in Trouble: Plagiarism, Fraud, and Politics in the Ivory Tower.* New York: New Press, 2005, chap. 11.

Woodmansee, Martha, and Peter Jaszi, eds. *The Construction of Authorship: Textual Appropriation in Law and Literature.* Durham, N.C.; London: Duke University Press, 1994.

A NOTE ON THE TYPE

THIS BOOK WAS SET in Monotype Dante, a typeface designed by Giovanni Mardersteig (1892–1977). Conceived as a private type for the Officina Bodoni in Verona, Italy, Dante was originally cut only for hand composition by Charles Malin, the famous Parisian punch cutter, between 1946 and 1952. Its first use was in an edition of Boccaccio's *Trattatello in laude di Dante* that appeared in 1954. The Monotype Corporation's version of Dante followed in 1957. Although modeled on the Aldine type used for Pietro Cardinal Bembo's treatise *De Aetna* in 1495, Dante is a thoroughly modern interpretation of the venerable face.

Composed by Creative Graphics
Allentown, Pennsylvania
Printed and bound by R. R. Donnelley and Sons
Crawfordsville, Indiana
Designed by Virginia Tan